Amelia mixed the mustard

Amelia mixed the mustard

and other poems.

selected and illustrated by
Evaline Ness

Charles Scribner's Sons, New York

ACKNOWLEDGMENTS

"Abigail" by Kaye Starbird: From "Abigail" from *The Pheasant on Route Seven* by Kaye Starbird. Copyright © 1968 by Kaye Starbird. Reprinted by permission of J. B. Lippincott Company.

"Adventures of Isabel" by Ogden Nash: From "The Adventures of Isabel" from *Many Long Years Ago* by Ogden Nash. Copyright 1936 by Ogden Nash. Reprinted by permission of Little, Brown and Co.; also by permission of The Estate of Ogden Nash and J. M. Dent & Sons Ltd.

"Amelia Mixed the Mustard" by A. E. Housman: From *My Brother, A. E. Housman* by Laurence Housman. Reprinted by permission of Charles Scribner's Sons. Copyright 1937, 1938 Laurence Housman; also by permission of the Society of Authors as the literary representative of the Estate of A. E. Housman, and Jonathan Cape Ltd., publishers of *A.E.H.* by Laurence Housman.

"Eat-It-All Elaine" by Kaye Starbird: From *Don't Ever Cross a Crocodile* by Kaye Starbird. Copyright © 1963 by Kaye Starbird. Reprinted by permission of J. B. Lippincott Company.

"Girls' Names" by Eleanor Farjeon: From *Poems for Children* by Eleanor Farjeon. Copyright 1933, © renewed 1961 by Eleanor Farjeon. Copyright 1951 by Eleanor Farjeon. Reprinted by permission of J. B. Lippincott Company; also by permission of Harold Ober Associates Incorporated.

"Harriet Hutch" by Laura E. Richards: From "Nonsense Verse" from *Tirra Lirra* by Laura E. Richards, published by Little, Brown and Company.

"I Am Rose" by Gertrude Stein: Reprinted from *The World Is Round*, text © 1966, by Gertrude Stein, a Young Scott Book, by permission of Addison-Wesley Publishing Company.

"I Would Like You for a Comrade" by Edward Abbott Parry: From *Katawampus* by Edward Abbott Parry. Used with the permission of Christy & Moore Ltd.

"Pandora" by Myra Cohn Livingston: From *The Malibu and Other Poems* by Myra Cohn Livingston (A Margaret K. McElderry Book). Copyright © 1972 by Myra Cohn Livingston. Used by permission of Atheneum Publishers; also by permission of McIntosh and Otis, Inc.

"Poem for Flora" by Nikki Giovanni: From *Re: Creation* by Nikki Giovanni, copyright © 1970 by Nikki Giovanni. Reprinted by permission of Broadside Press and Nikki Giovanni.

"Portrait by a Neighbor" by Edna St. Vincent Millay: From *Collected Poems* by Edna St. Vincent Millay, published by Harper & Row. Copyright 1920, 1948 by Edna St. Vincent Millay.

"Rebecca" by Hilaire Belloc: From *Cautionary Verses* by Hilaire Belloc. Published 1941 by Alfred A. Knopf, Inc. Reprinted by permission of the publisher; also by permission of A. D. Peters and Company.

"The Quiet Child" by Rachel Field: From *Poems* by Rachel Field. Reprinted with permission of Macmillan Publishing Co., Inc. Copyright 1924, 1930 by Macmillan Publishing Co., Inc.

"Where's Mary?" by Ivy O. Eastwick: From *Fairies and Suchlike* by Ivy O. Eastwick. Copyright, 1946, by E. P. Dutton & Co., Inc., publishers, and used with their permission.

To females all: Big, Little & Middle

Contents

AMELIA MIXED THE MUSTARD

Amelia mixed the mustard,
    She mixed it good and thick;
She put it in the custard
    And made her Mother sick,
And showing satisfaction
    By many a loud huzza
"Observe" said she "the action
    Of mustard on Mamma."

A. E. HOUSMAN

EAT-IT-ALL ELAINE

I went away last August
To summer camp in Maine,
And there I met a camper
Called Eat-it-all Elaine.
Although Elaine was quiet,
She liked to cause a stir
By acting out the nickname
Her camp-mates gave to her.

The day of our arrival
At Cabin Number Three
When girls kept coming over
To greet Elaine and me,
She took a piece of Kleenex
And calmly chewed it up,
Then strolled outside the cabin
And ate a buttercup.

Elaine, from that day forward,
Was always in command.
On hikes, she'd eat some birch-bark
On swims, she'd eat some sand.
At meals, she'd swallow prune-pits
And never have a pain,
While everyone around her
Would giggle, "Oh, Elaine!"

One morning, berry-picking,
A bug was in her pail,
And though we thought for certain
Her appetite would fail,
Elaine said, "Hmm, a stinkbug."
And while we murmured, "Ooh,"
She ate her pail of berries
And ate the stinkbug, too.

The night of Final Banquet
When counselors were handing
Awards to different children
Whom they believed outstanding,
To every *thinking* person
At summer camp in Maine
The Most Outstanding Camper
Was Eat-it-all Elaine.

KAYE STARBIRD

IF NO ONE EVER MARRIES ME

If no one ever marries me—
    And I don't see why they should,
For nurse says I'm not pretty
    And I'm seldom very good—

If no one ever marries me
    I shan't mind very much;
I shall buy a squirrel in a cage,
    And a little rabbit hutch.

I shall have a cottage near a wood,
    And a pony all my own,
And a little lamb, quite clean and tame,
    That I can take to town.

And when I'm getting really old,
    At twenty eight or nine,
I shall buy a little orphan girl
    And bring her up as mine.

LAURENCE ALMA-TADEMA

MEG MERRILIES

Old Meg she was a gypsy;
    And lived upon the moors:
Her bed it was the brown heath turf,
    And her house was out of doors.
Her apples were swart blackberries,
    Her currants, pods of broom;
Her wine was dew of the wild white rose,
    Her book a church-yard tomb.

Her brothers were the craggy hills,
    Her sisters larchen trees;
Alone with her great family
    She lived as she did please.
No breakfast had she many a morn,
    No dinner many a noon.
And, 'stead of supper, she would stare
    Full hard against the moon.

But every morn, of woodbine fresh
    She made her garlanding,
And, every night, the dark glen yew
    She wove, and she would sing.
And with her fingers, old and brown,
    She plaited mats of rushes,
And gave them to the cottagers
    She met among the bushes.

Old Meg was brave as Margaret Queen,
    And tall as Amazon;
An old red blanket cloak she wore,
    A chip-hat had she on.
God rest her aged bones somewhere!
    She died full long agone!

JOHN KEATS

PANDORA

There's this thing about Pandora's box.
This wondering. This curiosity.
There it was, this box,
Not locked or anything.

And Pandora was bored.

You've heard the rest.
She opened it.
Out came everything bad—
Evil, Famine, Crime, War, Greed
In a great black cloud.

The only joker in the lot was Hope.

MYRA COHN LIVINGSTON

GIRLS' NAMES

What lovely names for girls there are!
There's Stella like the Evening Star,
And Sylvia like a rustling tree,
And Lola like a melody,
And Flora like a flowery morn,
And Sheila like a field of corn,
And Melusina like the moan
Of water. And there's Joan, like Joan.

ELEANOR FARJEON

I WOULD LIKE YOU FOR A COMRADE

I would like you for a comrade,
    For I love you, that I do,
I never met a little girl
    As amiable as you;
I would teach you how to dance and sing,
    And how to talk and laugh,
If I were not a little girl
    And you were not a calf.

I would like you for a comrade,
    You should share my barley meal,
And butt me with your little horns
    Just hard enough to feel;
We would lie beneath the chestnut trees
    And watch the leaves uncurl,
If I were not a clumsy calf
    And you a little girl.

EDWARD ABBOTT PARRY

I love you

ADVENTURES OF ISABEL

Isabel met an enormous bear,
Isabel, Isabel, didn't care.
The bear was hungry, the bear was ravenous,
The bear's big mouth was cruel and cavernous.
The bear said, Isabel, glad to meet you,
How do, Isabel, now I'll eat you!
Isabel, Isabel, didn't worry;
Isabel didn't scream or scurry.
She washed her hands and she straightened her hair up,
Then Isabel quietly ate the bear up.

Once in a night as black as pitch
Isabel met a wicked old witch.
The witch's face was cross and wrinkled,
The witch's gums with teeth were sprinkled.
Ho, ho, Isabel! the old witch crowed,
I'll turn you into an ugly toad!
Isabel, Isabel, didn't worry;
Isabel didn't scream or scurry.
She showed no rage and she showed no rancor,
But she turned the witch into milk and drank her. . . .

OGDEN NASH

MS. MINNIE McFINNEY, OF BUTTE

Ms. Minnie McFinney, of Butte,
Fed always, and only, on frutte.
    Said she: "Let the coarse
    Eat of beef and of horse,
I'm a peach, and that's all there is tutte."

ANONYMOUS

REBECCA, Who Slammed Doors for Fun and Perished Miserably

A Trick that everyone abhors
In Little Girls is slamming Doors.
A
Wealthy Banker's
Little Daughter
Who lived in Palace Green, Bayswater
(By name Rebecca Offendort),
Was given to this Furious Sport.

She would deliberately go
And Slam the door like Billy-Ho!
To make her Uncle Jacob start.

She was not really bad at heart,
But only rather rude and wild:
She was an aggravating child . . .

It happened that a Marble Bust
Of Abraham was standing just
Above the Door this little Lamb
Had carefully prepared to Slam,
And Down it came! It knocked her flat!

It laid her out! She looked like that.

aggravating child!

Her funeral Sermon (which was long
And followed by a Sacred Song)
Mentioned her Virtues, it is true,
But dwelt upon her Vices too,
And showed the Dreadful End of One
Who goes and slams the door for Fun.

HILAIRE BELLOC

I AM ROSE

I am Rose my eyes are blue
I am Rose and who are you?
I am Rose and when I sing
I am Rose like anything.

GERTRUDE STEIN

I am Rose

THE QUIET CHILD

By day it's a very good girl am I;
I sit by the fire and sew,
I darn the stockings and sweep the floors
And hang the pots in a row.
But, oh, by night when the candle's out
And my bedroom black as pitch,
I've just to crackle my thumbs to turn
Into a wild bad witch.

Nights of storm and nights of stars
Are all the same to me—
It's up on my broom and straddle the wind
As it whips my pigtails free.
Over the chimney pots to go,
Past the jumbled lights of towns,
With the hosts of good black trees beyond,
And dim sheep-sprinkled downs.

No one knows when morning comes
And I'm back in bed once more,
With tangled hair and eyes a-blink
From the sunshine on the floor—
No one knows of that witch who rode
In the windy dark and wild—
And I let them praise my sober ways,
And call me a quiet child!

RACHEL FIELD

JUMPING JOAN

One-ery, two-ery, ziccary, zan;
Hollow bone, crackabone ninery ten;
Spittery spot, it must be done;
Twiddleum twaddleum Twenty one.
Hink spink, the puddings stink,
    The fat begins to fry,
Nobody's at home, but jumping Joan,
    Father, mother and I.

MOTHER GOOSE

and I

POEM FOR FLORA

when she was little
and colored and ugly with short
straightened hair
and a very pretty smile
she went to sunday school to hear
'bout nebuchadnezzar the king
of the jews

and she would listen

shadrach, meshach and abednego in the fire

and she would learn

how god was neither north
nor south east or west
with no color but all
she remembered was that
Sheba was black and comely

and she would think

i want to be
like that

NIKKI GIOVANNI

like that

35

PORTRAIT BY A NEIGHBOR

Before she has her floor swept
    Or her dishes done,
Any day you'll find her
    A-sunning in the sun!

It's long after midnight
    Her key's in the lock,
And you never see her chimney smoke
    Till past ten o'clock!

She digs in her garden
    With a shovel and a spoon,
She weeds her lazy lettuce
    By the light of the moon.

She walks up the walk
    Like a woman in a dream,
She forgets she borrowed butter
    And pays you back cream!

Her lawn looks like a meadow,
    And if she mows the place
She leaves the clover standing
    And the Queen Anne's lace!

EDNA ST. VINCENT MILLAY

GREEDY JANE

"PUDDING *and* pie,"
Said Jane; "O my!"
"Which would you rather?"
Said her father.
"Both," cried Jane,
Quite bold and plain.

ANONYMOUS

ABIGAIL

Abigail knew when she was born
Among the roses, she was a thorn.
Her quiet mother had lovely looks.
Her quiet father wrote quiet books.
Her quiet brothers, correct though pale,
Weren't really prepared for Abigail
Who entered the house with howls and tears
While both of her brothers blocked their ears
And both of her parents, talking low,
Said, "Why is Abigail screaming so?"

Abigail kept on getting worse.
As soon as she teethed she bit her nurse.
At three, she acted distinctly cool
Toward people and things at nursery school.
"I'm sick of cutting out dolls," she said,
And cut a hole in her dress, instead.
Her mother murmured, "She's bold for three."
Her father answered, "I quite agree."
Her brothers mumbled, "We hate to fuss,
But *when* will Abigail be like us?"

Abigail, going through her teens,
Liked overalls and pets and machines.
In college, hating most of its features,
She told off all of her friends and teachers.
Her brothers, graduating from Yale,
Said: "Really, you're hopeless, Abigail."
And while her mother said, "Fix your looks,"
Her father added, "Or else write books."
And Abigail asked, "Is that a dare?"
And wrote a book that would curl your hair. . . .

KAYE STARBIRD

Is that a dare?

QUEEN NEFERTITI

Spin a coin, spin a coin,
    All fall down;
Queen Nefertiti
    Stalks through the town.

Over the pavements
    Her feet go clack,
Her legs are as tall
    As a chimney stack;

Her fingers flicker
    Like snakes in the air,
The walls split open
    At her green-eyed stare;

Her voice is thin
    As the ghosts of bees;
She will crumble your bones,
    She will make your blood freeze.

Spin a coin, spin a coin,
    All fall down;
Queen Nefertiti
    Stalks through the town.

ANONYMOUS

WHERE'S MARY?

Is Mary in the dairy?
Is Mary on the stair?
What? Mary's in the garden?
What is she doing there?
Has she made the butter yet?
Has she made the beds?
Has she topped the gooseberries
And taken off their heads?
Has she the potatoes peeled?
Has she done the grate?
Are the new green peas all shelled?
It is getting late!
What? She hasn't done a thing?
Here's a nice to-do!
Mary has a dozen jobs
And hasn't finished two.
Well! here IS a nice to-do!
Well! upon my word!
She's sitting on the garden bench
Listening to a bird!

IVY O. EASTWICK

HARRIET HUTCH

Harriet Hutch,
Her conduct was such,
Her uncle remarked it would conquer the Dutch:
She boiled her new bonnet,
And breakfasted on it,
And rode to the moon on her grandmother's crutch.

LAURA E. RICHARDS

About the Illustrator

The honesty, humor, and vitality of Evaline Ness's art work have brought her wide acclaim and popularity as a children's book illustrator. She is the winner of the Caldecott Medal for *Sam, Bangs and Moonshine*, which she wrote and illustrated, and three of her books—*Tom Tit Tot, Pocket Full of Cricket*, and *All in the Morning Early*—were selected as Caldecott Honor Books. Two of Ms. Ness's most recent books are *Yeck Eck*, which she wrote and illustrated, and *Old Mother Hubbard and Her Dog*. Ms. Ness was born in Ohio and studied art at the Chicago Art Institute, the Corcoran Gallery of Art in Washington, D.C., and the Accademia di Belle Arti in Rome.

About the Authors

The poems in this collection come from the past and the present and cover a broad literary spectrum—light verse, limerick, lyric, and traditional. And, all reflect the poets' understanding and appreciation for the individuality of women. From the poignancy of Alma-Tadema's "If No One Ever Marries Me," to the lyric portraits by Keats and Millay, to the simple joy of Stein's "I Am Rose" and Giovanni's "Poem for Flora," to the funny and outrageous defiance of Nash's "Isabel," Richards' "Harriet Hutch," and Housman's "Amelia," Evaline Ness has brought together a rich and varied collection that will have special significance for today's young reader.